# Apple Watch Series 6 User Guide

A Complete Manual for Beginners and Seniors
with Tips & Tricks to Learn How to Use the
Apple Watch Series 6 and WatchOS 7 Like A Pro

## Daniel Brent C.

# Table of Contents

# Introduction

The Apple watch has changed a lot over the years - there have been big updates and some smaller ones. But year after year, these updates combined have made the Apple Watch a must-have accessory you have to pair with your iPhone to make your life easier.

The Apple Watch Series 6 offers blood oxygen monitoring for the first time, a brighter always-on display, a faster battery charging capacity and a faster chip.

The Apple watch series 6 runs on the brand new watchOS 7 software that brings some useful tools, too, including Apple Watch sleep tracking with new watch faces and watch bands.

This book is a detailed, in-depth guide that will help you to maximize your Apple Watch Series 6 and WatchOS 7. It contains actionable tips and specific step-by-step instructions that are well organized and easy to read.

## What's new in Apple watch series 6

Apple packed a lot of new features into the Apple watch series 6. The top features of this new generation of Apple watch are highlighted below.

Brighter Display

Apple debuted the always-on retina display on the last generation of Apple watch. With the series 6, the display on the inactive state is brighter in brighter conditions.

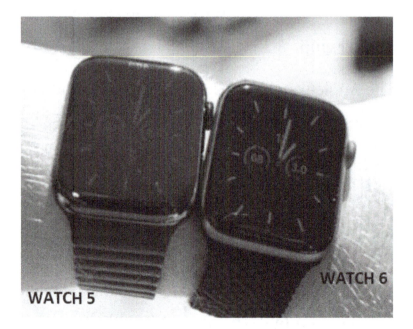

The new watch series 6 is brighter than the series 5 on their inactive states. Apple says the Series 6 is 2.5 times brighter than the previous generation.

<u>New colors</u>

The Apple watch series 6 comes in stunning new color options. Besides the silver, space gray and gold color options we've had on the apple watch for some years now, the aluminum series 6 also comes in two new colors.

A super sleek blue color and a sleek looking product red version.

Apple also did some tweaks to the stainless-steel finish. They added a new higher-end graphite color.

S6 SiP

The processing unit of the Apple watch series 6 is the S6 SiP (System in Package). It is built upon the A13 bionic processor but optimized for Apple watch and is 20 percent faster than the prior generation silicon.

Battery

The Apple Watch 6 still has an 18-hour battery life but can charge 20 percent faster. You can fully power your apple watch in one and a half hours.

<u>Wi-Fi</u>

Apple Watch has had Wi-Fi for years, but it was limited - it only worked with 2.4 Gigahertz networks. Now with the Apple watch series 6, it supports 5 gigahertz networks.

## Blood oxygen monitor

With the Apple watch series 6, we can now measure our blood oxygen level. The measurement takes only 15 seconds to complete, and it's a good measurement of overall wellness.

The new blood oxygen monitor built into the watch adds a new layer of vitals that the apple watch is able to capture on your wrist. Watch OS 7 introduces new sleep tracking and now with the series 6, we can take a blood oxygen reading within 15 seconds.

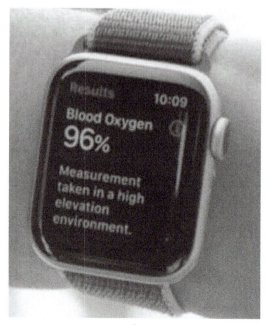

Health experts see blood oxygen as another important vital sign for the body and as the name suggests, this metric tells you how much oxygen your blood is currently carrying.

If you have low blood oxygen, you are going to experience signs like shortness of breath, rapid breathing, headache, etc. Therefore, it is nice that you can take this measurement on the apple watch especially if you need to keep track of your blood oxygen level.

**How to measure your blood oxygen level**

Set up the Blood Oxygen app using your iPhone

- Open the Apple Watch app on your iPhone. Your iPhone must be running iOS 14 or later if not, the blood oxygen app will not work.
- Tap "app view"
- Scroll down and tap Blood Oxygen
- Tap "Enable"

- Complete the setup by following the instructions displayed on your screen.

**Note**: The Blood Oxygen app won't be available if you set up your Apple Watch with Family Setup,

<u>To measure your blood oxygen level:</u>

- Ensure your Apple Watch Series 6 is snug and on the wrist you selected in the Apple Watch app.

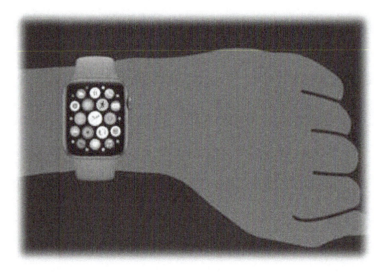

- Open the Blood Oxygen app on your Apple Watch.

- Keep your wrist flat with your Apple Watch facing up, and stay still
- Tap "Start"

**Note**: The measurement takes 15 seconds to complete and it's best to rest your arms on a table or on your lap during this time. Once it's complete, you'll receive your results.

- Tap Done to finish.

## Altimeter

The altimeter on the Apple watch series 6 gets an upgrade. With the 6th generation apple watch, the altimeter is able to run the entire time in the background.

It can detect elevation changes down to a single foot which will come in handy during exercises and to constantly track your elevation during hiking.

## Chapter 1: Setting Up and Getting Started

Before we get started with this guide, let's see how the apple watch looks and then note its important features.

## The Home button

The home button is fixed to the right panel of the watch.

- Press the Home button once to go to the home screen of the watch.
- If you press it twice, you will be taken back to the previous application you were working on.
- If you press the button for as long as five seconds without taking off your hand, you will be directed to Siri, your assistant.
- To zoom into the screen or scroll up or down the display, turn the power knob.
- When you press the home button for long, you will also see a feature that allows you to place your device on Power Reserve mode.

## The Side button

This button is just below the home button.

- If you press this side button, you can hide or show your friends.

- Pressing down on the button twice will lead you to Apple Pay.

- To power, your device on or off, press the button down for as long as five seconds without taking your handoff.

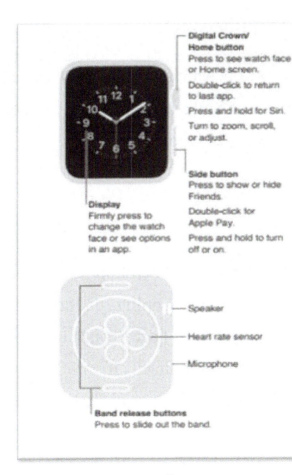

## The Display

The display is manipulated by the touch screen of the Apple watch.

Tap the screen and hold on to the gesture for long to switch the display to something else.

## The Back of the watch

At the Back of the watch, you will find a speaker, heart rate sensor and a microphone. The speaker resembles two closely joined lines.

## Gestures

The Apple Watch, unlike iPhones, respond to more gestures than swiping or tapping the screen. With the aid of a Force Touch technology, the watch can steer itself to work just by detecting the pressure you apply to the screen.

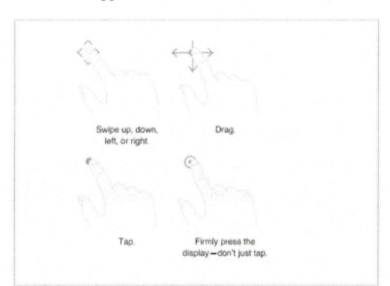

For example, you can run your finger across the screen to either swipe up, down, left or right. You can also hold on to a widget for some time and then, drag it to any position on the screen.

## How to set up your Apple Watch

The major setting up of your Apple watch involves you pairing it with your iPhone device. Only a few iPhone operating systems (iOS 8.2 and other higher software updates) are compatible with the Apple watch. So, if yours is any lower, kindly update the software before continuing with the steps below:

- Ensure that your device is well charged.
- On the compatible operating systems, you will find an icon that talks about the Apple Watch application. So, on your iPhone device, turn on the Apple Watch application.
- Strap your watch about your wrist and then, press the side button to power on the watch.
- On the display, you will see the Apple logo.
- Use your other hand to position your iPhone device above the watch.
- On the iPhone device is a software that finds other devices with the camera. Use this application to find your Apple Watch on your iPhone device.
- Follow the on-screen instructions displayed on your iPhone device to continue the set-up on it.

- Select your language.

- Select the orientation you want the watch to be in, i.e. portrait or landscape.

- Type in the Passcode you want your watch to respond to.

**Note**: Having the Apple Watch sit firmly on your wrist will give it maximum levels of efficiency.

## Icons on the status bar

The status bar is the section of the display of your Apple watch that provides you with all the information you need on about your watch. Let's run through a few of the things you might see.

- A red circle shows that you have a new notification.

- A small icon of lightning shows that your device is charging.

- The icon of a padlock shows that the watch has been locked.

- The icon of a crescent shows that your watch is on the 'Do not Disturb' mode. This mode is one that will prevent calls, messages any other network connection from showing on your display. However, your alarms will still ring out.

- The icon of a plane shows that your device is on the Airplane mode. This way, you won't be able to access anything that has to do with the internet. However, other applications will still work.

- When the connection between your watch and iPhone device has been severed, you will see an icon of a phone with a bar drawn diagonally across its surface.

- A circle of dots show that an activity is going on on the watch.

## Chapter 2: The Apple Watch application

This application is found on your iPhone. The function of this application is to let you do things that you cannot do on the watch. Examples of such things include the customizing of your settings, the setting up your Apple Pay account on your apple watch etc.

Also, this application becomes very useful when you want to download and install application software on your Apple watch.

### How do you open this application?

- On your iPhone device, tap the 'Apple Watch App' icon.

- Tap the 'My watch' icon.
- You will then see a list of the settings that manipulate your watch.
- Navigate from that screen.

## How to wake and unlock your Apple watch

- To wake your Apple watch, elevate your wrist and then, tap the screen display.
- When you depress your hand, the Apple watch sleeps.
- In a situation where the watch is not strapped to your wrist, press down on the home button to wake up the device.

In a situation where your watch does not wake up when your wrist is elevated, ensure you chose the right orientation options on the settings you did on the iPhone device. Go to the 'Digital Crown orientation' icon to tamper with the settings.

Another cause could be your device having a flat battery.

## How to make your watch wake to the feature you were working on before it slept

The Apple watch was set to a default that returns the watch to the watch face when you wake it up. To alter this, follow the procedures below.

- Tap the 'Settings' icon.
- Tap the 'General' icon.
- Tap the 'Activate on Wrist Raise' icon.
- Tap the toggle switch to turn it on.
- Go back to the 'Activate on Wrist Raise' icon.
- Under the options you see there, tap the 'Resume Previous Activity' icon.

## How to Unlock your watch

This procedure will have to be done on your iPhone device if your device gets unlocked with the aid of a passcode.

- On your iPhone device, tap the 'Apple Watch application' icon.
- Tap the 'My watch' icon.
- Tap the 'Passcode' option.
- Tap 'Unlock with iPhone'.

To do this from your Apple watch, follow the procedure below:

- Tap the 'Settings' icon.
- Scroll down the screen of the watch and tap the 'Passcode' option.
- Tap the 'unlock with iPhone' toggle switch to turn the feature on.

**Note**: Your Apple Watch will ask for a passcode shortly after you unhook it from your wrist or loosen the straps.

## How to change the Passcode of your Apple watch

- Tap the 'Settings' icon on your Apple watch
- Run you finger up the screen to access the other features below.
- Tap the 'Passcode' feature.
- Tap 'Change Passcode'

A few instructions will be displayed across your screen.

- Type in a new four-digit code.
- Type it in the confirmation bar again.

To change your Passcode with your iPhone:

- Tap the 'Apple Watch app' icon.
- Tap the 'My watch' icon.
- Tap the 'Passcode' icon.
- Tap the 'Change Passcode' icon.
- Follow whatever on-screen instructions that appear on your screen shortly after.

## How to type in a password longer than the usual four digits

- Tap the 'Apple Watch app' on your iPhone device.
- Tap the 'My watch' icon.
- Tap the 'Passcode' icon.
- Tap the 'Simple Passcode' toggle to turn the feature off.
- You can now set your Passcode to something longer.

## How to turn off the Passcode feature

- Tap the 'Settings' icon on your Apple watch.
- Tap the 'Passcode' icon.
- Tap the 'Disable Passcode' icon.

To do this with your iPhone device:

- Tap the 'Apple Watch app'
- Tap the 'My watch' icon.

- Tap the 'Passcode' option.
- Tap the toggle switch for the 'Turn Passcode off' feature to turn it off.

**Note**: Turning off the Passcode feature will disallow you from using the Apple Pay application on your Apple Watch.

## How to lock your Apple watch automatically

- On your iPhone, tap the 'Apple Watch application' icon.
- Tap the 'My watch' icon.
- Tap the 'General' icon.
- Tap the 'Wrist Detection' icon to turn on the feature.

**Note**: If this feature is turned off, you will not be able to use the Apple Pay application.

## How to lock your device manually

- Press the side button for a long time.
- Across your screen's display, you will see some slides.
- Shift the 'Lock Device' slide to the right side of the display.

## How to wipe off all data files from your Apple watch

To protect your files, you can set your Apple watch so that in a case where your Passcode is typed in wrongly ten times, all your files will be erased. In case your watch is stolen, you can also wipe your data files off your Apple Watch from your iPhone

- Tap the 'Apple Watch application' icon.
- Tap the 'My watch' icon.
- Tap the 'Passcode' icon.
- Tap the 'Erase Data' icon.

## Adjust Brightness

- Tap the 'Settings' icon.
- Scroll up the screen and then, tap the 'Brightness and Text Size' icon.
- Tap the brightness icon which resemble the figure of the sun.
- To increase or decrease the brightness of your display, press the home button.

To do this on your iPhone:

- Tap the 'Apple Watch app'.
- Tap the 'My watch' icon.
- Tap the 'Brightness and Text Size' icon.
- Move the small ball-like control horizontally to adjust the brightness.

## How to increase the size of the text on your device's display

- Tap the 'Settings' icon.

- Tap the 'Brightness and Text Size' icon next.
- Tap the 'Text size' icon.
- Tap the 'letters' icon. You could also use the home button to increase or decrease the size of fonts.

To do this on your iPhone device:

- Tap the 'Apple watch app' icon on your device.
- Tap the 'My watch' icon.
- Tap the 'Brightness and Text size' icon.
- You will see a slide bar next. Drag the ball-like knob to increase or decrease the size of the font.

## How to make the text of your device bold

- Tap the 'Settings' icon.
- Tap the 'Brightness and Text Size' icon.
- Turn on the switch for 'Bold Text'.

- After turning on the bold text feature, your Apple watch will reset in line.
- Tap the 'Continue' icon.

## How to adjust the sound of your device

- Tap the 'Settings' icon.
- Tap the 'Sounds and Haptics' icon.
- Tap the slide bar and drag the knob to increase or decrease the volume of the sound.

You can also control the volume of the sound from your iPhone:

- Tap the 'Apple Watch application' icon on the display of your device.
- Tap the 'My watch' icon.
- Tap the 'Sounds and Haptics' icon.
- Move the slider under that icon to decrease or increase the sound's volume.

## How to mute your Apple watch

- Tap the 'Settings' icon.
- Tap the 'Sounds and Haptics' icon.
- Switch on the 'Mute' feature.

To do this on your iPhone:

- Tap the 'Apple Watch application' icon.
- Tap the 'My watch' icon.
- Tap the 'Sounds and Haptics' icon.
- Turn on the 'Mute' icon.

## Cover to mute

Another alternative to muting your device is by placing your palm on the display screen and leaving it there for as long as five seconds.

Once you feel a vibration run through your hand, you can take your palm off. It signifies that you have successfully muted your watch. But then, before this method of muting your device can work, make sure that you must have allowed it in the settings on your iPhone device.

- To do that, tap the 'My watch' icon under the Apple Watch application and then, tap the 'Sounds and Haptics' icon.
- Tap the 'Cover to Mute' menu option.

## How to adjust the haptic intensity of your Apple watch

When your watch receives notifications, alerts or messages, it causes a vibration to run through your wrist. You can tone down the degree of these vibrations though.

- Tap the 'Settings' icon.
- Tap the 'Sounds and Haptics' icon.
- Beneath the section for 'Ringer and Alert' Haptics, tap the haptic icons.
- To adjust the intensity of the haptic vibrations, turn the home button in a screw manner. When you turn it clockwise, the intensity increases and when you turn it anticlockwise, the intensity drops.

To do this on your iPhone device:

- Tap the 'Apple Watch app' icon.
- Tap the 'My watch' icon.
- Tap the 'Sounds and Haptics' icon.
- Drag the slide ball for the 'Ringer and Alert Haptics' to reduce or increase the intensity. Dragging it forward increases it while you are dragging it backward decreases the intensity.

## Do not Disturb

The 'Do not disturb' option is another way by which you can mute your Apple watch. This way, all calls, messages and alert you receive will not light up the display of your device. However, this does not stop alarms from ringing out at their set time.

*How can you turn on this feature?*

- Swipe up the screen of your device.

- Tap the 'Settings' icon.

- Tap the 'Do not disturb' icon.

- Turn on the toggle switch for the 'Do not disturb' icon. The blue crescent at the status bar shows that you have succeeded in turning the feature on.

## How to silence both your iPhone and Apple watch at the same time

- Tap the 'Apple watch app' icon on your Apple watch.

- Tap the 'My watch' icon.

- Tap the toggle switch to turn on the 'Do not disturb > Mirror iPhone.

With this feature, when you turn on the 'Do not Disturb' mode on your Apple Watch, the one on your iPhone will automatically be turned on too.

## How to change language of your device

- Tap the 'Apple watch application' on your iPhone device.
- Tap the 'My watch' icon.
- Tap the 'General' icon.
- Tap the 'Language and Region' icon.

## How to change the wrist and Home Screen orientation

If you decide to start wearing your Apple watch on a different hand or plan on making the Home button do different tasks, you should try out the following procedures.

- Tap the 'Settings' icon.
- Tap the 'General' icon.
- Tap the 'Orientation' icon. Under this, you will find one that at ends to the wrist and another that attends to the crown.

- To change the orientation on your iPhone, tap the 'Apple Watch application'.

- Tap the 'My watch' icon.

- Tap the 'General' icon.

- Tap the 'Watch orientation' icon.

## Chapter 3: Power and Battery

### How to charge your Apple watch

- Position the Apple watch magnetic charger that came with your Apple watch on a regular and uniform platform.

- Plug the magnetic charger to the adapter you use for your iPhone device.

- Plug the adapter to a source of constant electricity supply.

- Place the back of the Apple Watch on the magnetic charger.

- You'll instantly hear a beep side from your watch as soon as the magnets in the charger align themselves properly with the magnets buried in the watch. The only time when you won't hear the beep is if your watch is muted.

- You will see the lightning icon on the display screen which means that the watch is charging. A green lightning icon shows that the device is indeed charging. The red lightning icon shows that you need to charge your device.

## How to check the remaining power on your Apple watch device

- Swipe up the display.

- Swipe to the display that shows the battery.

## How to merge the battery indicator of your device to the display screens of your Apple device

All the display screens—Modular, color, utility, simple, chronograph, mickey mouse—can have the battery indicators fixed to them. Follow the procedures below to make that happen.

- Tap the display of your screen for a long time.
- Tap the 'Customize' icon.
- Swipe your finger to the left till you get to a point where you can select the locations for each feature on your watch.
- Tap the location you want.
- Turn the home screen button around to select the 'Battery' icon.
- To exit, press the home screen button.

# How to use power reserves to make the available power last longer

Doing this will help your battery to last longer when it's low.

How? Your Apple Watch switches away from the full display of items and displays only the time, streamlining its functions solely to timing.

Follow the procedures below to start.

- Swipe up your display screen.
- Swipe over to the display that is meant for your watch's power
- Tap the 'Power Reserve' icon.
- Tap the 'Proceed' icon.
- You can also do this procedure alternatively by pressing the side button on your Apple watch till a slide bar shows up on your display.
- Drag the slider to the right.

Your device will automatically operate on the Power Reserve mode once the battery drops to something below 11 per cent. So, you do not need to put on this mode if your battery's full.

## How to return your battery to the normal power mode

If after setting your Apple watch on Power reserve mode, you change your mind and decide to get it back to the normal mode, how do you do it?

- Press the side button for a time long enough to get your watch to restart.

Before you can do this, you have to have enough battery on your watch first. Doing this without enough battery can lead to you having the same result when you eventually turn the watch back on.

## How to check the time since your last charge

- On your iPhone device, tap the 'Apple Watch app' icon.
- Tap the 'My Watch' icon.
- Tap the 'General' icon.
- Tap the 'Usage' icon.

This is where you can access how much time you spend using your watch and how long it stays on the standby mode. When you add the figures below this together, you will get to know when last you charged your device. For example, under 'Usage', you could see 50 minutes and then, under 'Standby', you could see 1 hour. What it means is that the last time you charged was an hour and 50 minutes ago.

## Chapter 4: Fundamentals of the Apple Watch

### How to arrange applications on your Apple watch

The Apple Watch has a lot of applications that work for a variety of purposes like keeping you informed, in touch and on time! You will find all of this application software clustered into a circle on your Home screen. If you don't like the way they are clustered together, you can just rearrange them!

But then, before we go to such depths, let's learn some of the basics.

## How to open an application

To open an application, you have to see it.

From the display screen that shows the time, press the Home screen button. This tap will lead you to the home screen of your device. Tap the icon of the application you want to open and voila, you have it done!

To open the application at the center of the home screen, turn the home button around.

## How to go back to the application you were using previously

To return, all you need to do is press down to the home button twice.

## How to return to the display of your watch that shows the time

To return, tap the 'Watch' icon on the home screen of your watch.

## How to rearrange your applications

- On your Apple Watch, press the Home screen button to go to the home screen.
- Tap any app you want to move and hold on to the tap until you see the apps there move about shortly in a frenzy.
- Drag the application to the new location of your choice.
- After moving the app, press the home button of your watch.

To do this on your iPhone:

- Tap the 'My watch' icon.
- Tap the 'App Layout' icon next.
- Tap and drag the application to a new location.

- If you end up wanting to get the arrangement back to the way it originally was, tap the 'Reset' icon. This way, every displaced application bounces back to where it came from.

## How to find and install applications from the App Store

- On your iPhone, tap the 'Apple watch app' icon.
- Tap the App Store to access the applications that are compatible with your Apple watch.
- You can either buy or download a list of applications on your iPhone device. Across the Apple watch's screen, you will see the pop up of a message that requires you to install the application to your device.

## How to adjust the settings for an application you just installed

- On your iPhone device, open the 'Apple watch app.'
- Tap the 'My watch' icon.
- Scroll down your screen to access your applications.
- To alter the settings, tap any of the settings available.

## How to check the storage used by an app

- On your iPhone, tap the 'Apple Watch application.'
- Tap the 'My watch' icon.
- Tap of the 'General' icon.
- Tap the 'Usage' icon. Under this icon, you will get to know the amount of space each application uses. You can also check for the amount of space left on your Apple watch.

# How to hide an installed app from Apple watch

- Press the home button to go to the home screen.
- Press any application for long until you see the 'X' sign at the upper lines of the app.
- To delete the application from your Apple Watch, you can tap the 'X' sign.

However, the application you delete will still exist on your iPhone device. It will only be gone if you delete it from your iPhone too.

## To show or hide apps

- Tap the 'Apple Watch app' on your iPhone device.
- Tap the 'My watch' icon next.
- Scroll up the screen of your device to access the applications you installed on your Apple watch at one point or the other.

- Once you find the application, tap the name.

- Tap the 'Show app on Apple watch' icon.

Any application that was installed on your Apple watch when you bought it cannot be hidden.

## How to stay up with friends

To have a view of the people you would like to stay in contact with the most, use the side button of your Apple Watch device. This feature allows you to call and message your friends easily only when you add them to your iPhone device.

## How to add friends to your iPhone

Your Apple watch usually scours your iPhone device for twelve of your favorite friends on your contact list, and then adds them up to the Apple watch automatically.

If you, however, feel that the device made a few wrong choices, you can change what you see on the Apple watch. Follow the steps below to do that.

- Tap the 'Apple Watch app' icon on your iPhone.
- Tap the 'My watch' icon.
- Tap the 'Friends' icon.
- In the list of friends that you see, tap the 'Add friend' icon.
- You will see a long list of your friends just then. Tap the name of your friend when you see it.
- In case you don't find the contact you are looking for, leave that page, go to the 'Contact' application on your iPhone and then, add your friends again from there.

## How to see your friends on your Apple Watch

- Press the side button.
- You will see at most twelve of your favorite friends.
- To choose a friend, roll the home screen button either in clockwise or anticlockwise moments.
- Select how you want to hook up with that friend.

## How to use the 'Handoff' feature to shuttle between your iPhone and your Apple watch

On your Apple Watch, the Hands-Off feature allows you to work on both of your Apple devices, with you still having a grasp on what you are doing. Let's cite an example. You can decide to scan through your emails on your Apple watch and reply to the ones that need responses on your iPhone.

*How do you activate this amazing feature?*

- Wake your iPhone.
- At the lower-left corner of the lock screen of the device, you will see an icon that tallies with the app you were formerly working on your Apple Watch.
- Swipe up across that icon and then, reply the email message.

However, it's not all the applications on your Apple watch that can respond to the Hands-off feature. Only applications like Mail, Maps, Messages, phone, reminders, Calendars, and Siri can. Also, know that this feature will not work if there is a large distance between your iPhone and your Apple watch.

## How to turn the Handoff mode on your Apple Watch on/off

- On your iPhone, tap the 'Apple Watch application'.
- Tap the 'My watch' icon.

- Tap the 'General' icon.
- Enable the 'Handoff' feature.

## How to locate your iPhone with your Apple watch

Your house could be so big that you could lose your iPhone somewhere within a bundle of pillows or something. Do not fret! Your Apple Watch will do the job of finding your device!

To ping your iPhone:

- Swipe up on the display that bears the time and then, swipes across the screen to the part that bears the 'Settings'.
- Tap the 'Ping iPhone' option.

However, if your iPhone is not somewhere close to you, you can find it by using the 'Find my iPhone' feature on iCloud.com.

## How to use your Apple Watch without the iPhone device it was paired with

The Apple Watch takes a better form and performs many other functions when your iPhone is in close range. But then, what happens if it isn't? Does Apple watch cease to exist?

No! Even without the iPhone device, you can still operate other functions.

- Once you are synced with a playlist on your Apple Watch, you can play music. Your Apple Watch has a loudspeaker.

- The Apple Watch is a modified form of a watch, so, of course, you still should be able to handle things like alarms, timers and stopwatches even without the iPhone device.

- With the 'Activity' app, you can keep track of your activities.

- You can also manage your workout sessions on the track with just your Apple Watch.

- You can display your pictures across the screen once you are synced with a photo album on your device.

- You can work with Apple Pay.

The Apple Watch connects to the paired iPhone through wireless technology. So, for operations that require wireless activity, it uses your iPhone for it.

If your Apple Watch and iPhone operate on the same network, but aren't linked with the Bluetooth technology, you can still do a few more iPhone independent operations.

- You can send and receive messages via iMessage.

- You can send and receive messages via Digital Touch.

- You can also work with Siri!

## Siri on the Apple Watch

Even on your Apple Watch, Siri remains as helpful and informative as always.

## How to ask Siri a question

- Raise your wrist, tap the screen, wake up your Apple Watch.
- When the display brightens, say this, 'Hey, Siri,' followed closely by the command you want to give to the software.
- You can also activate Siri by pressing the Home button until you see a sign that your device is listening to you at the bottom of your screen.
- Say your command and then, take your finger off the Home Screen button.
- To give a reply to something Siri said to you, keep on pressing down on the Home screen button and speak.

## What do you do to your Apple Watch when you are just about to fly?

If you are going to keep either your iPhone or Apple Watch on while staying in an airplane, do well to turn on the 'Airplane mode' of the devices so that you don't mess with the signals of the aeroplane.

## How to turn on Airplane mode

- Swipe up the display that gives the time on your watch.
- Swipe across the screen until you reach the display for your device's settings.
- Tap the icon for the 'Airplane mode'. The icon resembles an aeroplane.
- At the status bar, you will see in red prints the word, 'Disconnected.'
- You can also turn on the Airplane mode of your device through the settings.
- Tap the 'Settings' application.

- Tap the 'Airplane' mode.

Once the mode is successfully activated, you will see the icon for the mode at the status bar of the display.

## How to place both your iPhone and Apple Watch on Airplane mode at the same time

- Tap the 'Apple Watch app' on the iPhone device.
- Tap the 'My Watch' icon.
- Tap the 'Turn on the Airplane Mode > Mirror iPhone'.

If you want to switch off the Airplane mode though, you might have to do that separately on each device.

## Chapter 5: Watch Faces

### How to customize your watch face

Customizing the face of your watch will give you the ability of making the display look just the way you want it to look. You can also customize it to stock the home screen with important features you know you'll need. You can change colors, features, display designs and every other thing you might want to change.

### How to change the watch face

- When your Apple Watch is showing the display with the time, tap the screen's display for long.

- You will see a lot of already designed watch faces.

- Swipe until you find the one that pleases you and when you do, just tap on it.

- You can also add to the watch face additional features by tapping the 'Customize' feature just below the watch.

- That way, you can access other information like weather details and stock price along with the time.

## How to add a watch face to your collection of custom faces

- When your Apple Watch is showing the display with the time, tap the screen's display for long.

- You will see a lot of already designed watch faces.

- Keep swiping across the screen until you reach the end of the designs. There, you will see the '+' icon. Tap it.
- To browse through designs, swipe up and down across the screen.
- Tap the design you want to add to the watch faces available.
- After adding it, you can take a step further by getting it customized.

## How to delete a face from your collection of watch faces

- When your Apple Watch is showing the display with the time, tap the screen's display for long.
- You will see a long list of watch faces. Swipe across the screen until you find the one that you don't want again.
- Swipe that particular one up and tap the 'Delete' icon.

## How to get the time on your watch to be more advanced

- Tap the 'Settings' application on your Apple Watch.
- Tap the 'Time' icon.
- Tap the '+0 minute' icon.
- To set the watch at a different pace of 59 minutes, turn the Home Screen button.

These advanced settings do not affect your Alarms or the time that the notification on your device works with. It also doesn't affect the world clock.

## Some Watch Faces and their Features

Astronomy

This face shows you the picture of the solar system, the position of the sun and the moon. It also displays the current day, date and time.

On the face, you will see the icon of a crescent. Tap it to see the form the moon is in at that moment.

## Chronograph

This watch face measures the time in certain increments, just like an analogue stopwatch would do.

The chronograph face can also be activated right from the watch face and you can adjust the color of the face and the details of the dial.

You can add dates, calendars, moon phases, sunrise phases, weather phases, stock phases, alarm phases, timer phases and the world clock phase.

## Modular

This watch face has an adjustable design face that allows you to chip in a lot of features that will only give you better details of how your day is going.

## Motion

This watch face displays vibrant designs like those of butterflies, flowers or fishes.

## Simple

This face may seem to be very normal, but then, the face remains as attractive as it should be.

## Solar

This watch face displays the position of the sun in the sky, basing its view on your location and time.

On this face, you can also see additional features like the day, date and time at that moment.

## Utility

This watch face is characterized by three clock hands that move around the figures— very realistic. You can add more features to the face.


## X-Large

This particular watch face displays the time in extremely bold figures.

## Chapter 6: Notifications

A few of the notifications you may receive on your Apple Watch include invitations to meetings, messages, reminders, alarms and so on. The moment your Apple Watch received a notification, it gets displayed across the screen at once. Even if you don't check them immediately, you can check them later as they'll be saved up for you to access.

### How to respond to a live message on your Apple Watch

- If you feel a buzz against your wrist, it is probably a notification.
- Elevate your wrist to view it.

- To find the bottom of the notification, you can turn the home screen button.
- Tap the icon you see there.
- You could also open the application from which the notification is being received by tapping the icon at the very top.

## How to dismiss a notification

- Swipe to the bottom of the notification by turning your home screen button.
- Tap the 'Dismiss' icon.

## How to select the notifications you receive on your Apple watch

- On your iPhone, tap the 'Settings' icon.
- Tap the 'Notification' bar.
- There, mark the kind of applications that should generate notifications on your device.

- From there, head over to the 'Apple Watch app' on your iPhone device.
- Tap the 'My Watch' icon.
- Tap the 'Notification' bar.
- Tap the application whose notifications you want to be getting.
- Tap the 'Mirror my iPhone' icon.

If you want to browse through a different set of notification settings than the ones on your iPhone, tap the 'Custom' icon instead.

## How to silence notifications

- Swipe up on the watch face.
- Swipe across the screen till you get to the Settings.
- Tap the 'Silent mode' icon.
- To change the vibration you feel when a notification arrives, put your watch on the 'Do not Disturb' mode.

## How to keep your notifications private

When your notifications pop up on your screen, you will first see a concise explanation of what the notification is about. After a few seconds, you would see the rest of the details, i.e. who the message is from, then the actual message.

To stop all of this information from flaring across your watch's screen, follow the procedures below.

- Tap the 'Apple watch app' on your iPhone.
- Tap the 'My Watch' icon.
- Tap the 'Notification' icon.
- Turn on the toggle switch for 'Notification Privacy.'

## How to respond to unread notifications

The notifications that your Apple watch receive are usually stored on the device when you don't check them. You will find all of the messages in the notification center of your Apple Watch.

When you see a red dot at the status bar of your Apple Watch, it means that you have a notification you haven't checked.

To access the notification, swipe down the screen of your Apple watch. If you have tons of notification, you can scroll through them by swiping your finger up and down the screen. You could also turn the home screen button to either go up or go down the list.

## How to clear notifications on your Apple Watch

What your Apple Watch does is to remove a notification from the list of messages once you view it. But, how can you delete the message?

Swipe your finger across the screen in the left direction. After that, you will see a screen display with the 'Clear' icon. The message will get deleted immediately.

If you, however, want to delete all the notifications from your Apple Watch, tap the screen and keep your finger on it for a long time. Tap the 'Clear all' icon.

## Chapter 7: Glances

You will need to focus on this area if you want to get a concise briefing on important information right from the Apple watch's face. You can also have details or summaries of the application you use frequently. To do this, follow the procedures below.

- Swipe up on the face of your Apple Watch to see the 'Glance' display.

- Swipe either to the left or right to view all glances.

**How to check your glances on your Apple Watch**

- Swipe up on the watch face to view the glance you viewed last.

- Then, swipe either to the left or to the right to view other glances.

- Swipe down to return to the normal Watch display.

**If you need additional information about your Apple watch than the one your glances are giving you:**

- Tap the glance to open the related application.

**How to pick your glances**

- Tap the Apple Watch app on your iPhone.

- Tap the 'My Watch' icon.

- Tap the 'Glances' icon.

You can also choose to remove or add glances to your Apple Watch. With this procedure, you will be only able to see what you want to see; it depends on you.

**Note**: You can't remove the settings glance.

## How to set your glances in order

- Tap the Apple Watch application on your iPhone device.
- Tap the 'My Watch' icon.
- Tap the 'Glances' icon.
- To rearrange the glances, drag your finger across the screen.

## Timekeeping features

With this feature, you can set the time in other cities of the world, set alarms, use timers and also, use a stopwatch. You can add these elements to your watch face of your Apple watch too so that you can see them quickly when you need to.

## Chapter 8: Time

**How to check the time in other locations**

The World clock app on your Apple Watch enables you to check the time in different cities across the globe.

- Open the application to check times at different locations. For example, you can check what the time is in Auckland.
- You can also add cities to your watch face for quick reference.

**How to check the time on your device when you are in another city**

- Tap the 'World clock' app on your Apple Watch.

- Turn the home screen button.
- Swipe the screen to scroll through the list of cities on your Apple Watch.

If you have a city whose time you would like to see, you can add the world's clock to your watch face and choose the city whose time you want to be displayed.

## How to see information about the city

You can check the time the Sun rises and sets in the city you are in.

- Tap the city you are in on the World Clock list.
- Then tap the '<' icon on the upper left side of your screen's display.
- Swipe right across your screen's display to return to the city list.
- Press the home screen's button to return to the watch's face.

- When you add a city on the World Clock, the cities you add on your iPhone will also appear on your Apple Watch's world clock.

- Tap the Clock app on your iPhone device.

- Tap the 'Add' button icon. The icon is represented by this icon— (+). You can type in the city's name or scroll up the list.

## How to add a world Clock to your Apple watch's face

You can add a World Clock to the different Watch faces of your device. Some watch faces on your Apple Watch will enable you to add more than one world clocks.

- Firmly tap the display screen.

- Tap the 'Customize' icon.

- Swipe to the left until you can choose the features of the watch faces on your Apple Watch device.

- Tap the one you would like to use for a World Clock.

- Then, turn the Home screen button to choose a city.

- When you are done, press the home screen button.

You can add a world Clock to these faces: Chronograph, Color, Mickey Mouse, Modular, Simple and utility. The watch face shows the time in the city you choose.

## How to change the abbreviations of the different cities on your Apple Watch

- Open the Apple Watch application on your iPhone device.

- Tap the 'My Watch' icon.

- Then, go to the 'Clock > city abbreviation' icon.

- Tap any city to change its abbreviation on your Apple Watch device.

## How to set Alarms on your Apple Watch

- Use the alarm clock app to play a sound.

- The Apple watch will vibrate at the right time for the alarm.

Note: You can also add an alarm to your watch face so that you can see upcoming alarms at a glance. You can also open the Alarm clock app with a single tap.

## How to add an alarm to your Apple Watch

- Open the Alarm clock application on your Apple Watch.
- Firmly press the display screen of your device.
- Tap the New icon on your display. A cross sign represents the New icon.
- Tap the 'Change Time' icon.
- Tap the 'a.m.' or 'p.m.' icon.
- Tap the 'hours' icon or 'minutes' icon.
- Turn the home screen button to adjust the time.
- Then tap the 'Set' icon.

- Tap the '<' in the upper left corner of your screen to return to the alarm settings.

- Then, tap the 'Set', 'Repeat', and 'Label' and 'Snooze' icon to adjust to your suiting.

## How to set or adjust an alarm on your Apple watch

- Open the Alarm clock application.

- Tap the alarm in the list to change its settings.

- Tap the toggle switch next to the alarm icon to either turn it on or off. For example; you can turn off the alarm you set to sixty-thirty.

- You can tap the 'Edit Alarm' features to correct things.

## How to see upcoming alarms on the Apple Watch face

- Tap the Display screen of your Apple device.

- Then tap the 'Customize' icon
- Swipe to the left until you can choose individual watch face features.
- Tap the watch face you'd like to use for alarm.
- Press the home screen button.

**Note**: You can add alarms to these faces: Chronograph, Color, Mickey mouse, Modular, Simple and utility.

- When an alarm sounds, you can tap the 'Snooze' icon and wait for several minutes before the alarm sounds again.
- However, if you don't want to allow the 'Snooze' feature, you can work around it.
- Tap the alarm in the list of alarms.
- Then tap the 'Snooze' icon and then, turn off the feature.

# How to delete an alarm from your Apple watch

- Tap the 'Alarm Clock' icon on your Apple device to turn it on.

- Tap the alarm in the list you see on the next page.

- Scroll to the bottom of the display screen.

- Then tap the 'Delete' icon to delete the alarm.

# How to use the 'Timer' on your Apple Watch

The timer app on your Apple Watch will help you keep track of time. You can also set the Timer for 24 hours. For example, you can set Timer for 30minutes.

# How to set the 'Time' on the Timer application of your device

- Tap the 'Timer' icon on the home screen of your device.
- Tap the 'hours' icon or the 'minutes' icon.
- Turn the home screen button to adjust the time on your timer app.
- Tap the 'Start' icon.

## How to set the Timer for more than 12 hours

- Press the display for long.
- Then, tap the' 24-hour' icon to increase the time rate of the Timer.

## How to add the 'Timer' feature to the Watch face of your Apple Watch

- Press the display
- Then, tap the 'Customize' icon.
- Swipe to the left until you can choose the individual face features on your Apple device.

- Tap the one you'd like to face you would like to see for your Timer.
- Then, turn your Home screen button to highlight and choose the Timer.
- Press the home screen button.

## How to switch the stopwatch on/off

- Open the stopwatch app on your Apple Watch device.
- Tap the stopwatch on your Apple Watch face.

## How to start, stop or reset the time on your stopwatch

- Tap the 'Start' icon.
- Tap the 'Lap' icon to record a lap or split in time.
- Tap the 'Stop' icon' to record the final time set.

- Tap the 'Reset' icon or the 'Lap' icon to reset the stopwatch settings.

## How to choose the stopwatch format

- Tap the display while the stopwatch display is showing.
- You can tap either the 'Analog', 'Digital', 'Graph,' or 'Hybrid' icons.

## How to switch between analogue 1-dials and analogue 3-dials with splits on your Apple device

- Swipe up on the 1-dial analogue stopwatch display to see minutes, second, and tenths dials above a scrolling list of lap times.

## How to monitor timing on your Apple Watch

- Add a stopwatch to the face.

- Your current elapsed time will be visible on the face of your watch.

- Tap it to switch to the stopwatch app.

- Check for your lap times on your Apple device.

## How to quit using the stopwatch

- If you are using the stopwatch app, Press the home screen button.

- If you are using the Chronograph watch face, tap the 'Lap' icon to reset.

## Chapter 9: Digital Touch

This feature allows you to send your sketch outlines and heartbeat to your friends. It works by detecting the amount of pressure you exert on the display of your watch's screen. However, for the transfer to be successful, your friend has to have an Apple Watch.

**How to open Digital Touch**

- Tap the side button of your Apple Watch to view your friend list.
- Tap the friend you want to send the sketch to.
- Beneath the picture of your friend, you will see the Digital Touch icon.

- Tap that icon.
- The only reason you will not see the icon is probably that your friend does not own an Apple watch.
- To know the tips and techniques that aid the Digital Touch feature, tap the info. The icon on Digital Touch display.

## How to send a Digital Touch to your friend

- If you want to send a sketch to your friend, use two of your fingers to draw across the screen.
- To send to your friend, tap the screen of your Apple Watch once or twice. You could even create patterns with your taps.
- To send your heartbeat, place two of your fingers on the screen and keep them there until you see the animation of your heart on display.

## Chapter 10: Mails

### How to read your mails

- Tap the 'Mail' application on your Apple Watch device.
- To run through your list of mails, turn the home screen button either clock wisely or anti-clockwise.
- Tap any of the messages once to read the mail.
- To read the message on your Apple watch and then, type in the response on your iPhone device, go to its lock screen.
- At the bottom left corner of your device, you will see the 'Mail' icon. Tap it.
- Type in your response after doing that.

# How to read your emails right from the notification bar

If your Apple Watch has been programmed to display your mail notifications, you will be able to view your mails from the bar. If it isn't, you can handle it in the settings.

- Tap the 'Settings' icon.
- Tap the 'Notification on iPhone' icon.
- See if the toggle switch is on.
- Tap the mail notification if it was just got delivered to your watch. If it was delivered a long time ago, scroll up your screen to find it. You could also use the home screen button to scroll through the list of notifications.
- To dismiss the mail, tap the 'Dismiss' icon at the end of the message.

## How to flag your mails

- Tap the Display.
- Tap the 'Flag' icon.

- While you are observing the message list, swipe to the left side of the display and tap the 'More' icon.

- To flag the message when you read it in the notification bar, scroll to the Flag button at the end of the message bar.

- You can also remove the 'Flag' feature from the message.

## How to change the style of the flag on your Apple watch

- Tap the 'Apple Watch application' on your device.

- Tap the Display icon.

- Tap the 'Unread' or 'Read' icon.

- While looking at the list of messages, swipe to the left side and tap the 'More' icon.

## How to delete an email message

- Tap the display for a long time.

- Tap the 'Trash' icon.

- To delete the message, you can also swipe to the bottom of the message and then, tap the 'Trash' icon there.


## How to choose the mailbox that appears on your Apple Watch

- Tap the 'Apple Watch app' on your iPhone device.

- Tap the 'My Watch' icon.

- Tap the 'Mail' icon.

- Tap the 'Include Mail' icon.

You can select only one mailbox to appear on your Apple Watch's screen. If you don't do this, you will see details from all the mails on your Apple Watch.

## Chapter 11: Phone calls

### How to answer a Phone call

- The moment you feel the buzz that comes with an incoming call, elevate your wrist to see who is calling you.

- Tap the 'Answer' icon on your Apple Watch device.

- You can communicate with the caller by using your microphone and speaker.

If you, however, want to pick up the call with your iPhone device or type a text message, turn the Home Screen button to scroll down the page.

Choose whatever you want to do with the call from there. You can choose to hold the call, pick the call, bar the call, etc.

## How to place your call on hold on your Apple Watch

- Tap the 'Answer on iPhone' icon.
- Place the call on hold until you can get in touch with your iPhone device.
- Until you disable the 'Hold call' feature, the caller will continue to hear a continuous beeping sound.
- If you can't locate your iPhone device, tap the 'Ping' icon to locate it.

## How to switch a call from your Apple Watch to your iPhone

- On the lock screen of your iPhone, drag the icon you see at the bottom left corner.

- If your iPhone is unlocked, tap the green panel at the area of the status bar.

## How to adjust the volume of your call

- Turn the home screen button of your device.
- Tap the 'Volume' icon on the screen.
- If you are on a conference call, tap the 'Mute' icon to silence your side.
- To hastily silence any incoming call on your Apple Watch, you can press your palm to the screen to cover it. You can leave your palm there for about three seconds.
- But for the above function to work, you must adjust the settings on your iPhone.

## How to send a call to voicemail

- Tap the red icon on the display of your watch to decline the incoming call.

## How to listen to a voicemail

- You will receive a notification when a caller leaves a voicemail for you.
- Tap the 'Play' icon in the notification bar to listen to the voicemail.
- To listen to the voicemail at a later date, you can tap the 'Phone' application on your device and then, tap the 'Voicemail' icon.

## How to make calls on your Apple watch

- If the person you want to call is among the list of your favorite friends, press the side button of your device.
- You can also turn the home screen of your device to highlight a friend's name.
- Tap the 'Call' icon.

- If the person you want to call does not belong to your list of favorite friends, tap the 'Phone' application to place a call through to the person.

## Chapter 12: Apple Pay

Apple was able to develop a very wonderful way for the users of Apple devices to make contactless transactions. Apple Pay involves you withdrawing money for payments from a wallet that exists on your mobile phone. It is a very cool transaction process you cannot afford to miss! With this, you have your credit and debit cards tucked safely inside the folds of your online wallet.

You get to seal your payments in person or over the internet with your online wallets. This payment method is only supported by the Safari Browser. Do not worry, you have this browser on your iPhone devices.

So, you can use this technology to purchase application software, games, pay for pizza drop-offs and to buy your favorite Gucci shoes. Apart from these, you can use the online wallets to subscribe to apps like Apple Music, Apple News, and Apple Arcade. You probably do not need to carry real money around anymore!

## Banks and cards that work with Apple Pay

Apple Pay is compatible with credit and debit card producers like visa, master card, and American express. Do you know there is an Apple card too? Of course, it should not surprise us that this card is also compatible with Apple Pay.

## Where can Apple Pay work?

In places where contactless payments are allowed, you can easily make use of the Apple Pay technology. Another way you can know is by checking for an Apple Pay symbol. Any place where you see this symbol is sure to work with the technology.

And luckily for you, many places are now allowing the use of Apple Pay for payments. In the United States, Apple pay is allowed by about seventy-five percent of the stores. In the United Kingdom, Apple Pay is supported by over eighty percent of the stores. The highest support is offered by Australia which extends to a percent rate of ninety-four percent.

## Is there a limit for Apple Pay?

Most other card payments that require no contact usually would restrict you from spending nothing more than £45. However, Apple Pay does not place any restrictions on your spending. You can spend as much as you want, provided your wallet is stacked with enough money.

# What apps use Apple Pay for payments?

- Starbucks
- Deliveroo
- Apple Store.
- Uber and so on.

## Countries you can use Apple Pay

- The United States.
- The United Kingdom
- Canada
- Australia
- Hong Kong
- Japan
- China Mainland
- Iceland
- Macao
- New Zealand
- Singapore
- Taiwan
- Saudi Arabia
- Brazil
- Russia

- Spain
- Greenland
- Norway
- Netherlands
- Poland
- Romania
- Russia
- Serbia
- Spain
- Lithuania
- Jersey and so on.

## How to set up Apple Pay on your Apple watch

- First, you will need to get the Apple Wallet app on your device.

When you do that, set up the application. From the information required of you during this process, the wallet will keep records of the data on your credit and debit cards. So, when you make payments, the data records are pushed into actual effects by making the necessary withdrawals.

- On your iPhone, click the Wallet option in the app. That way, it will get it open.
- Next thing you will need to do is add credit and debit cards to the wallet. You will have to use the camera on your iPhone to record the information on the cards.
- Fill in any other information required of you.
- Any other verification you might need to do will be ones related to your bank(s). After your bank certifies the information you dropped above, you may have to make a few calls to them. If this doesn't happen, you may receive a message from your bank that contains a configured text code you will need for the verification.
- Well, all of the verification requirements rely heavily on the kind of bank you are using.

- Once the verification is over, click the 'Next' icon and begin to use Apple Pay's beautiful features.

## How to use Apple Pay on your Apple Watch

Apple pay needs a communication antenna (NFC), touch identification, or face identification.

- Double press the side button the left side of your Apple watch.
- Click the 'Pay with Passcode.' This feature works when your face is not recognized by the iPhone's sensor.
- After the authorization deal is over, your phone will say something. And that is 'Hold near Reader.'
- What that means is that you should position your device near a terminal aimed at contactless payments.

- A slight vibration of your watch validates the payment.
- On the Apple Pay Wallet app, you will see the receipt of your transactions.

With the above steps, you will notice that you do not have to turn on your phone's display or open any application. Every process has been neatly streamlined to facial recognition.

## How secure is Apple Pay?

Apple will never store the records of your payments and cash transactions. Even the figures on your card will be known by no one else but you! The only record of your payments kept at the ones you will see in the wallet app.

Apple explained to Apple Pay users that assigned, encrypted, and sealed in a small effective chip fixed inside your iPhone is your account number.

After any payment, the cashier or retailer you pay to receives his or her payments with no form of your card detail revealed to him or her. Yes, it is that safe.

## What happens to Apple Pay in cases of misplaced phones?

Since your payment transactions can only be completed with a thorough facial scan, anyone who picks up your Apple Watch cannot make payments with your wallet. The only exception to this is a situation where the individual knows your passcode text.

If that code is known by such a person, the only information they will be seeing is the last four digits on your cards and the address used for billing, nothing else.

There are some things you can do to protect your wallet though.

- On another iOS device, use the 'Find My Apple Watch' feature.
- Then, put your iPhone in lost mode.

This will lock everything on that lost device and consequently, ensure that not just anyone can view your Apple watch's content. So, that way, the data on your Apple Pay app will be kept safe.

You can also use that 'Find my Apple Watch' feature to completely erase your Apple Watch. This will be very necessary if you have more vital information on your device that is not just tied to Apple Pay

## The Apple ID, iCloud, and iTunes

Having an Apple ID is very necessary for an iPhone user. Without this identification, you cannot have access to services proffered by Apple. Examples of these services include

- Apple store

- Apple Arcade
- Apple Books
- Apple music
- Apple news
- Apple online store
- Apple podcasts
- Apple Pay
- Apple T.V
- Face time
- Apple channels
- iCloud
- iTunes
- Game centers and more...

When creating your iPhone's ID, you need to take note of everything you input in the bars. You will need them whenever you have to sign in to any Apple device. So, with that one account, you can access, manage, and control all your files. For your iPhone ID, all you need primarily is your email address and password.

## iCloud

You have to sign in here to view the following:

- Photos
- Videos
- Documents
- Notes
- Contacts and so on.

## Signing in to iTunes

You could see a message requiring you to sign in to iTunes.

*How do you get this done?*

- On the iPhone, click the 'Settings' icon.
- Sign in with your Apple ID.

• If you are using a Mac device, click the Apple menu, then, shortly after, click the 'System Preferences' menu option. Click the 'Apple ID' icon and then, sign in.

# Conclusion

The Apple Watch can be one of the best gadgets you own if you can take time to study the hundreds of amazing features that have been incorporated into it.

If you, however, have an issue with your Apple Watch device, report to any Apple Store instead of trying to fix it yourself.

Enjoy your time trying out your new Apple device!